It's Juz Biznuz

Ron Hine

Copyright © 2024 The HAHA Train

All rights reserved.

ISBN:

DEDICATION

This book is dedicated to all the workers of the world that, to survive, must get up every morning, grab your coffee, and band together to brave the peculiar alternate reality of the corporate world. Always remember, a company is the people who work there. Without them, it's just an idea.

BIZINTRO

I suppose it all began with that one ancient person who thought it was a good idea to trade a spear for some barosaurus meat. Oh, if they only knew what they would unleash. Today's corporate world rolls through our civilization like a giant machine that takes an army to operate and is barely under anyone's control. It creates products and services that transform our way of life. The jury is out on whether this transformation has improved our lives or just rearranged the furniture. None of this seems to matter. Nothing will stop us from showing up every day to carve off a piece of the beast for ourselves while we collectively make a lot of money for someone else. But it's all ok, and we can laugh at it, if we all keep one thing in mind. It's Juz Biznuz.

THE BUSINESS GOAL BLACKHOLE

It's the end of the year and time for your manager to set a new slate of business goals that are just outside of your reach! Business climate predictions are about as accurate as a long-term weather forecast so business goals can easily drown in the unexpected fiscal storms of the first quarter. No matter, tough goals are meant to help you grow (and your bonus to shrink).

SALES AWAY

Sales organizations are a separate company within a company. Corporate handbook? Who needs it. Sales navigates by their own stars! Salespeople are like a rushing river seeking the path of least resistance to get the sale. Yes, sometimes they flood the basement.

MAGIC MARKETING

If you walk through a marketing department, the first thing you'll notice is that no one's feet are touching the ground. The best marketing teams always seem to float in a parallel universe where everything is always beautiful, and your company's products and services are shielded from the nonsense of reality.

Marketing is the only business function that can take carbonated water infused with high fructose corn syrup, caramel color, a touch of caffeine, and a corrosive inorganic phosphorus containing acid, and sell 1.9 billion servings, every day (true story!).

Under the spell of Marketing's fantasy, it doesn't matter what your company sells. All that matters is what your customers think you sell.

"But your website said I was getting a wild and wet getaway to a tropical destination."

"All I got was a bottle of coconut water."

TECHNOLOGY TURMOIL

Tech departments are like the central nervous system in a company. When Tech Teams make mistakes, the company can end up in a lot of pain. Tech groups always seem to have biggest budgets and the best paying jobs. I guess the geek did inherit the earth (wasn't that supposed to be the meek?).

Software developers are the founders of the work-from-home movement. Once COVID ended, management went to great lengths to get them to come back and work from the office. Bless their little management hearts.

New Return to Office Work Policy

~~All employees must work in the office 5 days a week.~~ ~~3~~ ~~1~~

All employees must drive by the office once a month and wave like you mean it.

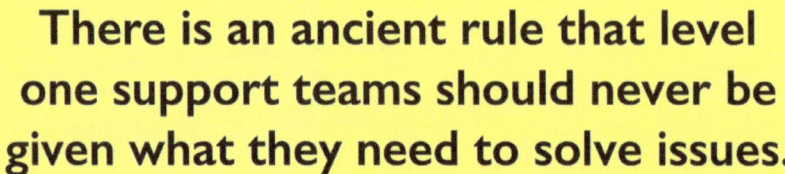

AI is sure to have an impact on the U.S. class structure.

Old US Class Structure

- Super Rich
- Rich
- Upper Class
- Middle Class
- Lower Middle Class
- Lower Class

New AI US Class Structure

- Super Rich
- Artificial Intelligence
- ✂
- Lolo Class

HUMAN RESOURCES TO THE RESCUE

Human Resources is a little like a Police Department in a company. They are the ones you go to for help but, there is a chance you'll get detained for a violated HR policy you forgot about. People management is the most difficult job in a company because, well, it involves people. And people do crazy things and have a difficult time agreeing on anything. Human Resources is probably not the right name. It's more like herding chickens. But you can't call it Chicken Resources. That would be an HR violation.

HR departments are always searching for the holy grail of performance reviews. Unfortunately, objectivity tends to be in the eye of the objector. When it comes to performance reviews, most managers and employees can agree on one thing, they hate them.

Some companies have wellness programs that are anything from a gym membership to forcing employees to have health improvement goals. You can recognize these efforts to control medical costs by their familer marketing label, "our corporate concern for healthy happy employees".

Historically, being able to work remotely has been a privilege for the few. COVID ripped a new one in that privilege and now working in the office is a punishment for the few. However, as attractive as it sounds, some people are not wired to work without the company of co-workers and the guardrails they provide.

HR will always publicly endorse a healthy work life balance. However, workers know that their boss thinks a healthy work life balance means the company will be healthier if your work is your life.

THE C-SUITE ELITE

The C Suite is that highest tower in the company castle. Very few people know what the C level executives do. All they know is that it involves meetings, decisions, meetings, presentations, meetings, meetings, and meetings. Workers typically think all the company crap rolls downhill from the C Suite to the rest of the company. All C Level execs know that the real bad crap rolls uphill. That's why their main job is hiring good crap catchers below them.

EOB-IZNUZ

With any luck, this book has enhanced your perspective of the business world but, probably not. Hopefully, it has at least increased your ability to laugh at it. As you steam ahead in your quest to meet that next deadline, don't forget to break out of the Circle of Work Life once in a while and smile. Life is much too short, and in the end, we eventually realize that success is measured in joy, not dollars. And besides, your co-workers could really use a smile and, you probably could too.

ABOUT THE AUTHOR

Ron Hine is the creator of the HAHA Train. After working almost forty years in the corporate world, he decided to retire to the business of humor. This is because, after all those years of chasing corporate goals, driving sales and marketing efforts, supporting technology, managing people, and working with the C-Suite, all he could do is laugh.

www.ingramcontent.com/pod-product-compliance
Lightning Source LLC
Chambersburg PA
CBHW040251220526
45473CB00001B/441